BIBLE CHARACTERS
IN POETRY

Leah Bethune Stevens

WESTBOW
PRESS
A DIVISION OF THOMAS NELSON

Graphics/art by Krohne Family Media.

WestBow Press books may be ordered through booksellers or by contacting:

WestBow Press
A Division of Thomas Nelson
1663 Liberty Drive
Bloomington, IN 47403
www.westbowpress.com
1-(866) 928-1240

ISBN: 978-1-4497-6025-0 (sc)

Library of Congress Control Number: 2012913150

Printed in the United States of America

WestBow Press rev. date: 07/27/2012

DEDICATION

Dedicated to Mike, Sharon and Janet, three of the greatest joys God has given me this side of heaven.

My Dearest Friend

May I introduce you to my dearest friend
I met many years ago?
Through the years, I've cherished this friend.
Even today I depend on and love this friend so.
This friend has never spoken an unkind word,
nor has ever put me down.
This friend has always put a smile on my face;
Even on the days I feel to frown.
This friend is not only a friend in fine weather,
but has walked with me through life's storms.
When I contend with this world's cold realities,
this friend's love keeps me warm.
Oh, by the way, my friend's name is Jesus.
I know he would love to be a dear friend to you.
You'll never meet another
who would be a friend so faithful and true.

...and there is a friend that sticks closer than a brother.
Proverbs18:24

NOAH

"I'm Glad To Be On The Inside Looking Out"

There was a time when the Lord was grieved.
when he saw the wickedness of man.
So he said "I will destroy both man and beast,
that has populated the land;"
"Every creeping thing upon the earth,
even the fowl of the air;"
"For all the violence man has done,
is more than I'll forebear!"
But there was a man by the name of Noah;
a just and perfect man was he.
And Noah found grace in the eyes of the Lord;
because he walked before the Lord righteously.

God told Noah to build an ark of gopher wood,
and partition it within.
He gave him a set of blueprints,
on just how to begin.
The length was to be four hundred fifty feet,
and forty five feet high.
Noah knew if he built it God's way,
it would be a vessel on which he could rely.
Noah's massive ark was to be seventy five feet wide.
It had to be big enough to get all his family and animals inside.
Noah cut out a window underneath the roofline
for light all the way around.
He pitched it inside and out with tar,
to make its buoyancy sound.

The Lord said unto Noah, "Come into the ark.
Bring your wife, your sons, and your daughters-in-law;
It's almost time to embark.
Now bring the clean animals in by sevens;
bring the unclean in by two.
Bring of them, both male and female";
And Noah did all God commanded him to do.

God told Noah that it would rain
for forty days and nights.
But God made a covenant with Noah and all his house,
that he would see him through the awful plight.

So after they entered into the ark of safety,
God himself shut the door.
He had dealt with the wicked heart of man,
and he would deal with it no more.

As the waters increased and prevailed,
Noah could say without a doubt,
"It's so good to trust the Lord;
I'm glad to be on the inside looking out".

Jesus said, "As it was in the days of Noah,
so shall it be at the coming of the Son of Man";
For in the days before the flood,
they were consumed with their own plans.
They were unaware and unprepared,
until the day the flood swept across the land.

Even as it was then, so is it today;
many are unaware and unprepared,
for the coming of the Lord's great day.
And what are we doing to show these the way?

May we give heed to Noah's story;
it might be a lesson well learned.
Let us soberly and patiently watch,
for the Lord's return.
If Jesus is your ark of safety,
you can say without a doubt.
"I'm glad to be on the inside, looking out"!!

"Abraham"

"God Provided Himself A Lamb"

…And Abraham said,
"My son, God will provide himself a lamb."
Genesis 22.8

And it came to pass that God tested Abraham
to see what was in his heart;
For God said, "Abraham, take now your son,
into the land of Moriah apart."

"Upon a certain mountain
you will offer him, as a burnt sacrifice;
I will show you the one."
So Abraham rose up early, gathered the wood,
and took two young men, and Isaac, his son.

Now after a three day journey,
Abraham lifted his eyes to see;
the place afar off, that God had spoken of,
where the offering of his son would be.

No doubt Abraham must have had
many uncertainties in his heart to ponder;
Nevertheless, Abraham said to the two young men,
'Abide here, while I and the lad go worship yonder."

God had promised Abraham that Sarah would be
a mother of nations through Issac her son.
And kings would be born of his lineage;
Even Jesus, God's only begotten one.
And although Abraham did not understand
all that God would do,
Abraham knew that all God's promises
concerning his son were true;
So by faith Abraham declared to the young men,
"The lad and I will go, and return again unto you."

Abraham had to believe that God's grace would be sufficient;
his trust in God's providence could not lack;
So he took the fire in his hand, along with the knife,
and laid the wood upon Issac's back.

So up the mountain together as they progressed,
Abraham held fast to the promise concerning his son;
that in Issac, his seed would be called and blessed;
And everything promised to him would be done.

Issac asked, "Father, I see the fire and the wood,
but where is the sacrificial lamb"?
His father reassured him that the perfect sacrifice
would be provided by the Great "I am".

When they reached the place together
that God, to Abraham, had shown,
then Abraham built an altar
in preparation of giving his very own.

Abraham then bound Issac, whom he loved;
and laid him on the altar upon the wood.
He took his knife and stretched forth his hand,
and mustered up all the strength and courage he could.

Then the angel of the Lord called out from heaven.
"Stay your hand and do not harm your son.
For now I know that you fear me,
for you have not withheld your only one!"

Abraham lifted his eyes and looked behind
in a dense thicket of thorns;
and there he saw an offering for sacrifice,
a ram caught by his horns.

Abraham took the ram and offered him up,
instead of Issac, his son,
and called the place Jehovah-jireh,
and gave thanks for all God had done,

God did provide himself a spotless lamb,
one day on Calvary's hill;
so that mankind could be set free

from the bondage of sin,
according to his perfect will.
For he who knew no sin,
was made to be sin for you and me;
that we might be made the righteousness of God
and live eternally.

Joseph

In the Bible we find a very interesting story,
about Jacob's eleventh son.
The name that was given to this son was Joseph,
and he was Jacob's most beloved one;
Jacob loved Joseph above all his brothers,
because he was the son of his old age.
This put all of Joseph's brothers into a jealous rage.

Jacob made for this child a coat of many colors;
and this coat Joseph cherished and adored.
Joseph's brothers had a bitter resentment,
that each day grew more and more.
And there came a time when Joseph's brothers,
showed him just how much he was abhorred.

It came to pass, that Joseph dreamed a dream,
and he told it to his brothers.
He said, "We were binding sheaves in the field,
and lo, my sheaf arose and stood upright,
and to my sheaf, your sheaves began to yield,
and you all made obeisance before my sheaf,
and you all began to kneel."
The brothers exclaimed, "Who are you to think
that over us you will reign"?
And all Joseph's brothers treated his dream
with the greatest contempt and disdain.

But Joseph dreamed again,
and once again voiced it to his brothers.
He said, "I dreamed a dream,
much like the one before,"
"the sun and moon and eleven stars
made obeisance to me."
Now when the brothers heard this,
they hated him even more.

When Jacob heard about this dream, he rebuked his son,
"What is this dream that you have dreamed?"
"Do you think such a thing shall come to pass
and prove to be true"?
"Shall your mother, brothers and myself,
bow and make homage to you"?
Although Jacob did not understand,
why his son would dream such a dream,
he knew something about it could not be ignored.
From that day on, Joseph's brothers began to scheme;
for they despised and envied him even more.

On a certain day, Joseph's brothers went up to Shechem,
to feed their father's flock.
Joseph remained at home
to tend to the remaining livestock.
Now Jacob became worried over the welfare of his sons.
So Jacob sent Joseph out from the valley of Hebron,
to see if their jobs were being done.
When Joseph reached Shechem,
his brothers could not be found.
A man saw Joseph in the fields,
looking for his brothers all around.
The man told Joseph to go to Dothan,
and he would find his brothers there.
Now Joseph was glad when he finally found them;
but of the evil that awaited him he was totally unaware.
When Joseph finally reached his brothers,
they saw him afar off;
even before he came near.
They in unison began to mock and scoff;
"Behold the dreamer is here!"

They conspired together to slay him,
and to throw him into a pit.
"Let's kill the dreamer and his dreams will die."

The thought of killing their brother,
did not trouble them one bit.
They said, "We will tell Father
that he was devoured by a wild beast."
They had no compassion for their brother in the least.

When Reuben heard
what the brothers were planning to do;
he said, "do not kill him,
for innocent blood will be on your hands."
"Listen closely to me brothers,
for I have another plan."
So they stripped Joseph
of his coat of many colors,
and threw him into a darkened pit.
Reuben thought he would
secretly return to retrieve Joseph;
and that this foolish idea, his brothers would forget.

As the brothers sat down to eat and drink,
they saw a company of Ishmaelites,
carrying spices and myrrh into Egypt's land.
Judah questioned, "If we kill our brother,
how will we conceal the blood upon our hands"?
"After all, he is bone of our bone,
and flesh of our flesh."
So the brothers plotted to sell their very own.
They lifted Joseph from the pit,
and sold him to the Ishmaelites.
Twenty pieces of silver, they did get.

When Reuben returned to the pit,
Joseph could not be found.
Reuben rent his clothes in mourning
and fell weeping with his face to the ground.
He then arose and went back to his brothers,

to deliver the sorrowful news.
But they had already put their heads together,
to conspire the next evil they would do.
So they killed a goat,
and in its' blood,
they dipped Joseph's colorful coat.
They took the coat back to Jacob,
and when he saw it,
he was overcome with a horrible dread;
for he knew without a doubt,
that his beloved son was dead.
Jacob put on sackcloth and mourned many days.
And all his sons and daughters
could not comfort his heart in any way.

The Ishmaelites sold Joseph into Pharaoh's court;
to Potiphar, the captain of the guard.
The brothers of Joseph went on living their lives,
having for their brother no regard.
Now it was all over for Joseph,
or so it surely seemed.
Joseph's brothers were confident that their father
would never know about their little scheme.
They were sure they would hear no more
from the dreamer or his dreams.

So in Potiphar's house Joseph was a slave,
but Joseph had an excellent spirit,
and Potiphar saw, just how godly Joseph behaved.
The Lord was with Joseph,
and made all things to prosper in his hand.
Potiphar's entire house was blessed;
the cattle in the stall, the crops in the field
and all pertaining to his land.
So Potiphar elevated Joseph to overseer,
and Joseph was content in all his labors.

It was easy for the Egyptians to see,
that Joseph was a man well-favored.

It came to pass that Potiphar's wife,
tempted Joseph to a great sin.
She said, "come now and lie with me",
and this grieved Joseph within.
But she was head strong for his attention,
and tempted him day after day.
She stubbornly purposed not to stop,
until she got her way.
One day she caught Joseph at the house,
when her husband was not there.
She desperately grabbed him,
and his garment began to tear;
but he quickly ran out of it,
and fled, leaving it in her hand.
She was determined that he would pay dearly,
for rejecting her demand!
So she called for the other servants,
and spun them this great tale;
She said, "my husband's overseer tried to lie with me!"
She mustered up a few fake tears and then began to wail.

She kept Joseph's garment,
until her husband returned;
then she told a lie against Joseph,
because her attention he had spurned.
There is a saying,
as true back then as it is today,
"a lie will travel around the world,
before truth finds the way".

So Potiphar cast Joseph into prison,
and not one, who knew the truth, could be found.
His hands and feet were secured in the stocks,

where the king's prisoners were bound.
But the Lord was with Joseph,
and gave him favor, just as he had before.
The keeper of the prison committed
the care of all the prisoners into Joseph's hands.
The excellent reputation of Joseph
was noised throughout Egypt's land.

And it came to pass,
that Pharaoh's chief butler and chief baker,
had greatly offended and angered the king.
So Pharaoh put the two into the prison,
where Joseph was in charge of everything.
One night both the butler and baker had a dream.
The next morning they both were troubled,
for they could not find one who could interpret
the night visions, so it seemed.
Joseph asked, "why are you sad, today"?
"Why do you both fret"?
"Do not interpretations belong to God"?
"Tell me your dreams,
for my God has not failed me yet."

The butler began to tell Joseph his dream,
and this is what he said;
"There was a vine before me,
with three branches that budded and blossomed out.
This vine had clusters of ripened grapes.
It was a productive vine no doubt.
Now Pharaoh's drinking cup was in my hand,
and I pressed the grapes into cup.
Then when it was filled with the juice,
to the king I served it up."
Then Joseph began to interpret the dream,
and this is what he said;
"Within three days, this is what Pharaoh will do;

he will restore you back into your former place.
Please remember me, when it is well with you.
Please mention me before the king,
for the charges against me are not true."

Now the baker was anxious to hear
the interpretation of his dream.
He just knew his night vision had a good interpretation,
so with great excitement he began to beam.
He told Joseph that in his dream,
he had three white baskets on his head.
and in the uppermost basket,
for Pharaoh, there were baked meats and bread.
But the birds came down and ate them all.
When the baker had spoken this,
upon Joseph came an awful dread.
Joseph said to the baker,
"This is the interpretation of your dream.
It will be devastating for you to hear;
for this dream speaks of your impending death;
which is, according to the dream, very near.
Pharaoh will remove your head,
and hang you on a tree.
And the birds of the air will feast on your flesh;
in three days this shall be."

On the third day was Pharaoh's birthday.
Pharaoh restored the butler to his former place,
as he made for all his court a great feast.
The butler forgot Joseph back in the prison,
because he was not concerned about him in the least.
But the chief baker was hanged,
and his flesh was left for the birds and wild beasts.
As for Joseph, it looked as though
all hope was depleted;
but God was working, that his plan for Joseph

would be perfectly completed.

At the end of two years,
Pharaoh dreamed two dreams in the same night.
In the first dream, he stood by the river.
There came up seven cows out of the water,
and stood in plain sight.
These cows were fat, healthy and well-fed.
Then came up seven more cows,
sickly, lean and just about dead.
The sickly ones ate up the healthy;
then Pharaoh awoke, and tossed in his bed.

When Pharaoh was able to sleep again,
he dreamed another dream.
The second one was much like the first,
with the same meaning, so it seemed.
He dreamed that seven ears of corn, plump and good,
grew on the same stalk together.
Then appeared seven thin ears of corn,
blasted by the east wind and weathered.
The seven thin ears of corn devoured the good.

Then Pharaoh awoke,
and tried to understand what he could.
In the morning Pharaoh's spirit was troubled,
so he called in all the magicians and wise men.
Not one could interpret the dreams,
although he repeated them time and time again.

Then the chief butler remembered Joseph,
and quickly told the king.
Pharaoh immediately sent for Joseph,
in hopes that he could tell him the right thing.
When Joseph stood before Pharaoh,
Pharaoh said, "I have heard that you can interpret dreams."

"My magicians and wise men would not interpret,
and they have brought me much grief.
My dreams have troubled me and I need some peace.
Can you give me an answer, so I may have relief?"
Joseph said, "I cannot interpret,
but my God will interpret for you."
"Now O King, God was showing you through these dreams,
all he is about to do."
"There is coming seven years of great plenty,
throughout all of Egypt's land.
Then there shall arise a horrible famine
from God's own hand."

"Now O Pharaoh, find you a discreet and wise man,
who is able to devise a strategic plan;
to prepare Egypt for the famine,
that will surely consume the land."
"O King, lay up corn in abundance,
under the control of your mighty hand.
Set up officers throughout all of Egypt,
to gather in and store the fifth part;
So that when the famine comes,
there will be enough to eat,
and the people will not lose heart."

Pharaoh was at peace
with all Joseph had told him.
Pharaoh said unto his servants,
"this man Joseph, surely walks with God."
"I will set Joseph over all my affairs."
For Pharaoh knew wherever Joseph was,
his God's wisdom and honor was there.

So Pharaoh put a ring on Joseph's hand,
and a gold chain around his neck;
and over all Egypt, Joseph was second in command.

Pharaoh gave him a new name and a new wife,
and he diligently served all of Egypt's land.
Under Joseph's leadership, Egypt was made ready
for the famine that brought great devastation
to all the surrounding lands.
Many neighboring people began to hear,
how Joseph had prepared Egypt through God's prosperous hand.
For untold numbers, the famine brought a deadly dread.
But in Egypt's storehouses there was corn to make bread.

When Jacob saw there was corn in Egypt,
He said to his sons, "Go down into Egypt,
so corn you will be able to buy;
Do not stand there looking at one another;
hasten to do this so we can live and not die."
So ten of Jacob's sons left quickly for Egypt,
but Benjamin was left behind;
because they did not know
how Egypt would receive them;
or even if to them they would be kind.

Now when Jacob's sons arrived in Egypt,
Joseph was governor over all the land.
He was the one who proportioned the corn,
into the peoples' hands.
When Joseph's brothers came before him,
they bowed themselves to the earth.
Joseph immediately knew them,
but he wanted to see
what their intentions were worth.
So he made himself a stranger to them,
and spoke to them in a tone that was rough.
And for all the hard things they put him through,
he would make it a little tough.
He questioned them, "From where do you come,
and why are you here"?

The brothers answered, "We have come from Canaan,
to buy for our people some food."
Joseph declared, "Your real reason for being here,
before Pharaoh, must be proved."
"For you just want to see all we have in Egypt,
for you have been sent out as spies!"
"And now you stand before me,
to tell me all these lies!"

The brothers began to plead with Joseph,
"We have come to Egypt only to buy food;
we have told you no lies.
We are all the sons of one man,
we truly are not spies!"
"We have a younger brother at home with our father,
and a brother, whose whereabouts we are unaware."
Joseph demanded, "You shall not leave here then,
Until your younger brother comes hither."
The hope of Jacob's sons returning home,
was just about withered.
Joseph said, "Instruct one of them to go
back to your father's house,
the youngest to retrieve.
Bring him to me, that I may know you speak the truth;
and then all of you, I will believe."

The rest of his brothers were placed in the prison,
until the one brother could return.
Joseph longed to see his young brother;
and to have them all before him, he did yearn.
Joseph said "For now I will send you enough corn for
your father's people;
but be diligent to return the young one to me."
"I will then deal with you according to
just how much truth in you I see."
Now Joseph's brothers were beginning to wonder

if their sin against Joseph would soon find them out.
Would this governor over the land of Egypt,
find them to be true men, or would he have his doubts.

After three days in the prison ward,
Joseph came to his brothers again;
and said, "I will see just how honest you are;
I will allow you all to go but one."
"But if you do not return with the younger brother,
your father will be minus one son."
Joseph wanted to try them to see,
if they would have the same regard for a brother as before,
Would they show a great love and concern,
or would they be willing to mistreat another, even more.

Reuben spoke to his brothers
and reminded them, out of guilt and fear.
"Did we not see the anguish of Joseph's soul;
when he pleaded with us and we would not hear"?
"Now this difficulty has come upon us,
because of this great sin."
The more they reminded one another
of the deeds of the past,
the more their conscience troubled them within.
Joseph stood near and heard all they had to say.
His heart was broken all over again,
as he reflected on that awful day.
He turned aside and bitterly wept,
for his brothers he dearly loved.
His steadfast composure he bravely kept,
for he knew his strength came from God above.

Joseph took Simeon from among his brothers,
and bound him before their eyes
and carried him away.
Then Joseph commanded that his brothers' sacks be filled,

and provision be given for their journey,
without further delay.

Joseph also instructed,
that each man's money for the purchase of corn,
be restored into each sack.
Then they loaded the sacks filled with corn,
on all the animal's backs.
After leaving, one of the brothers,
opened his sack to feed his animal,
and found the money therein.
When they returned into Canaan,
they told Jacob all that had befallen them in Egypt,
and relived all that had happened to them again.
And when all the brothers opened their sacks,
and found their money,
they were sore afraid.
Then Jacob began to question them,
on how they had truly behaved.

When Jacob was told all concerning his youngest son, Benjamin,
he would not give him up, for fear he would be slain.
For he had lost one son already,
and that still brought his heart grievous pain.
But Reuben spoke up and said,
"Father, if I do not bring Benjamin back to you,
then slay my two sons in his stead."
But Jacob refused to let him go;
just the thought of it caused a horrible dread.

Now the famine remained in the land,
and the corn in Canaan was quickly consumed.
Jacob said, "Go back to Egypt and buy again."
But it would not be as easy as Jacob presumed.
Judah replied, "the lord of Egypt has strictly said,
we shall not see his face,

until we have brought our youngest brother.
And if we go without him, the trip will be a disgrace."

Judah pleaded with his father.
"let me take Benjamin with me,
or we shall surely die.
I will guarantee the life of Benjamin
with my own life;
On me you now must rely!"
Jacob replied, "If you must take Benjamin,
take also several gifts back to Egypt's land.
Take fruits, myrrh, honey and spices;
and be sure to take double the money in your hand.
Also take the money back that was in your sacks;
be sure to make that right.
For the lord of Egypt may think you stole the money,
or it may have been a serious oversight.
Now may God Almighty go with you and give you mercy.
I trust God to return all my sons to me;
for I cannot stand to lose another.
It would be too much, you see."

When the brothers once again stood before Joseph.
Joseph told the keeper of the house
to prepare a meal for noon.
Joseph's brothers wondered if this all was a plot,
and thought they might lose their lives soon.

As they stood in the threshold of Joseph's house,
they communed with their brother's steward.
They began to tell how they found
the money in all the sacks.
They said, "we have come to make sure
the money is given back."

"For we do not want to appear as thieves,

in your lord's sight.
Our father also told us that we must make
this misunderstanding right."

The steward said to them,
"Peace be to you, fear not.
Your God and the God of your father,
has given you treasure in your sacks.
I am the one that was put over your money,
to give your money back."
And when they turned and looked
Simeon stood before them all.
The brothers greeted him with gladness,
as the events of the past days,
to Simeon they recalled.

The steward welcomed the brothers in,
and gave them water to wash their feet.
Provision was given to the brothers' livestock,
and every need the steward was eager to meet.
When Joseph came in to dine with them,
he finally saw Benjamin, his mother's son.
He inquired, "is this your younger brother"?
He had trouble keeping his composure
until the introduction was done.
He immediately dismissed himself,
as his eyes filled with tears.
For his heart so desperately yearned
to draw his brother near.

After they had dined,
Joseph gave command to his steward,
that all the men's sacks be filled and restored.
But Joseph wanted to see if his brothers treated
the youngest any better than they had before.
His heart was very much endeared to them,

and had never been removed.
So he devised a plan,
so they might once again be proved.

The steward was instructed
to place the money back into the sacks.
But into the sack of Benjamin,
he was commanded to put Joseph's silver cup.
The steward could not understand,
but he knew something was up!
As the brothers left the city,
Joseph sent forth men after them,
and the brothers were overtaken.
When they heard the men's accusations of theft,
they knew without a doubt,
someone had to be mistaken.
The brothers said, "This makes no sense,
we gave back the money that we found!
We did not hold back what was not ours,
so for that reason this accusation isn't sound!
Now everything that we know,
we have truthfully told!
There is no reason why we would want to steal
any silver or gold"!

The brothers were brought back to Egypt
and when they saw Joseph,
they bowed themselves to the ground.
They could only hope and pray
that they all were not prison bound.
Joseph asked them,
"What deed is this that you have done"?
"For your youngest learned well from thieves"!
"I must deal severely with this one"!
"None of you can be believed"!
"And now your young one will serve me,
the remainder of his life.

Go and get you to Canaan,
before there is anymore strife."

Judah spoke up and said unto Joseph,
"My lord, of a truth I speak unto you,
for I cannot lie!"
"If we return home without our father's youngest,
then our father will surely die."
"If it please you my lord, take me as your servant
and I will do anything you say!"
But send the youngest back to his father,
so our father can live out his days."

Then Joseph could not refrain any longer,
But he said, "I am Joseph, also your father's son."
Immediately, they were troubled with all the memories,
of the evil they had done.

But Joseph reassuringly said,
"Do not be angry with yourselves;
let there be between us no strife."
"For I know of a certainty,
that God allowed all these things,
that he might preserve life."
"Now I have prepared a place in Goshen,
for all of you to dwell."
"There is still yet five more years of famine,
but in Goshen you and our father
will flourish well."
"Hasten now to Canaan to get our father,
whom I am so anxious to see.
Hurry back as quickly as you can,
that all my family may be with me."
Joseph fell on Benjamin's neck weeping,
and he kissed them all.
This was the happiest day that he could ever recall.

Moses And The Burning Bush

When Moses was at the backside of the desert,
tending to Jethro's flock,
He came upon the mountain of God,
and saw something that gave him quite a shock.
For there the angel of the Lord appeared,
in a flame of fire, out of the midst of a bush.
Moses knew right away it was a sight to be revered!
As he looked, the bush was not consumed,
though it burned with fire.
God knew just how to get Moses' attention,
for the situation back in Egypt was dire.

Moses was amazed to see, the bush was not burned,
and he heard a voice saying, "Moses, Moses"
Moses said, "here am I," as he slowly turned.
God warned Moses, "do not draw near,
but take your shoes from off your feet";
"For the place where you stand is holy ground."
Moses knew to be discreet.

The voice then said, "I am the God of your Fathers,"
and Moses hid his face.
For it didn't take him very long to realize,
he was in a hallowed place.
The Lord then reassured Moses,
"I've seen the affliction of my people, in Egypt's land".
"I've heard their cry by reason of their taskmasters,
and I am come down to deliver them from Pharaoh's hand."

"Now I will send you to Pharaoh's court,
that you may lead my children out.
You will not be alone, for I will be with you.
Trust me and do not doubt."

Moses pleaded,
"Who am I, O Lord, to do such a difficult task"?

"And who shall I say sent me"?
"For this they will surely ask."
God said, "Tell them I AM THAT I AM has sent you,
for this is my name.
This name shall be a memorial unto all generations,
for I am eternally the same."

"Furthermore, I will give my people favor
throughout Egypt's land."
"For when they leave the land of their bondage,
they will leave with great wealth in their hands.
Every woman shall borrow of her neighbor,
and they will freely give and not withhold.
My people will be given raiment and jewels,
and an abundance of silver and gold."

God said, "Go and I will do signs and wonders."
Moses began to reason and complain;
"the people will not hearken to my voice,
nor will they ever believe;"
"they will say you did not appear unto me,
and my words they will not receive."

The Lord said unto Moses,
"What is in your hand"?
Although Moses was confounded,
and could not understand,
he simply replied, "a rod".
It would not be long before he realized,
he had just met an awesome God!
For God said, "cast the rod to the ground";
it became a snake, and from it Moses fled.
Then the Lord commanded that he take it by the tail;
so Moses did as he was led.
The rod was instantly restored into his hand.
God said,"I am the God of Abraham, Issac, and Jacob.

All I have done here, I will do in Egypt's land."

God then commanded Moses
to put his hand into his cloak;
this he did, but Moses did not know,
that when he drew it out,
it would be leprous as snow.
Moses was amazed and wondered
what all of it was about.
God said, "put your hand into your cloak again,"
and it was restored when he drew it out.

God said unto Moses,
"If the people do not believe me,
after these things I do,
Then go down to the river,
and take a vial with you.'
"Pour out the waters,
and the water shall become blood upon the land."
If the people does not receive the first and second miracle,
maybe this one will cause them to understand."

Moses continued on
with the complaining trend.
Surely the Lord had to wonder
when all the griping would end.
But still Moses retorted,
"I cannot go and speak for you;
I am slow of tongue."
He had found so many reasons not to go,
before his journey had begun.

But the Lord patiently replied,
"I am he who made your mouth!"
"On this, do we not agree"?
Then if I am the one who made your mouth,

the one to fill it, will be me"!
Moses said,
"O, Lord instead of me, please send someone else;
this I humbly beseech.
There is no way I can do this, Lord!
Send someone who is eloquent in speech."

So the Lord told Moses, "Aaron is on his way;
and he will speak for you,
all the words I have to say."
"Go out to him and greet."
"Tell him all that I have told you,
when you two shall meet."

God said, "Go now, and I will be with you two,
and will teach you what to say."
"If you will trust and believe in me,
I will show you the way."
So Moses left from before the Lord,
not understanding how all this would be.
But he would have to trust in this awesome God,
and believe that all God had spoken, he would see.

"Samson"

In the days of the judges
Israel once again did evil,
in the sight of the Lord.
God dearly loved his chosen people,
but their sin he did abhor.
So he delivered them into
the Philistines' strong hand;
and for forty years,
they sorely oppressed the land.
Although this oppression was brought about
because of Israel's repeated sins,
God reached out with love and mercy
time and time again.

So, the angel of the Lord
appeared unto Manoah and his wife.
Although Manoah's wife was barren and could not bear,
the news the angel brought would change her life.
For the angel of the Lord declared,
"You shall conceive and bear a son.
He shall begin to deliver Israel;
and now according to the promise of God
will this thing assuredly be done."
At the appointed time Manoah's wife
brought forth a son and named the child, Samson;
and in the admonition of the Lord he grew.
But neither Manoah nor his wife,
understood the great feats he would do.

This child was not to be like any child;
this son would be a Nazarite unto God from the womb.
No razor was to come on his head,
and the fruit of the vine, he was not to consume.
For this child was to be consecrated
and separated unto a divine call.
And he grew in the purpose of the Lord,

and in the strength of the Lord, he stood tall.

Now the Philistines began to notice that in strength,
Samson superseded and surpassed;
by killing a young lion and walking off with the gates of the city,
and killing a thousand Philistines with a jawbone of an ass.
It came to pass that Samson loved a woman;
Delilah was her name.
But Samson was unaware
that this woman would bring him shame.
For the lords of the Philistines came to her and said,
"We will pay you well, to entice this one called Samson,
and see where his great strength lies;
that we may know how to bind and afflict him;
for this one we greatly despise."
So Delilah pleaded with Samson,
"Where does your great strength lie, tell me I pray."
Samson said, "Bind me with seven green cords,
and I'll be weak as any man and easily carried away!"
So Delilah bound him just as he had said,
and cried, "The Philistines be upon you,"
and he broke the cords like a thin thread.

Delilah said unto Samson,
"You have mocked me
and have tried to deceive!
Now if you tell me anything else,
how can I believe?"
So Samson said, "Bind me with new ropes
that have never been occupied.
Then you will see me as weak as any man,
and you will know I haven't lied."
So this Delilah did, just as Samson said.
But when she called out, "the Philistines be upon you",
he broke the new ropes as though they were a thin thread.

Delilah said, "once again you have mocked me."
"Nothing else you say, will I believe."
"For you will try to fool me yet again."
"I will not allow you to deceive."
So Samson said, "Weave the seven locks of my hair;
then I'll be as weak as any man,
just as I've declared!"
So as he slept, she fastened his head with a pin,
onto the weaver's beam.
It looked as though she finally had entrapped him,
or so it surely seemed.
But when she woke him from his sound sleep,
he walked off with the web and the pin of the beam.

So Delilah pressed on Samson
"Tell me about this great strength;
Tell me all, and nothing from me hide."
"How can you say you love me,
and you will not in me confide?"

So after certain days, the soul of Samson was vexed;
and what once seemed harmless,
now was greatly complexed.

So Samson began to tell Delilah all that was in his heart;
"I was born with a Nazarite vow,
and for God, I've been set apart."
"If I be shaven,
then my strength will go from me,
and I will become as weak
as any man, you see."
Delilah quickly realized
what Samson had said was true;
so she called for the lords of the Philistines,
and told them everything she knew.

They brought eleven hundred pieces of silver,
and placed it in her hands,
and as Samson slept upon her knees,
Delilah carried out her deceitful plan.
She called for one to shave off
the seven locks from his head;
And as soon as Delilah cried,
"The Philistines be upon you, Samson",
he awoke with a terrible dread!
The Philistines took him, and put out his eyes,
and bound him with fetters of brass.
They made him grind in the prison house,
and did awful things to harass.

But Samson's hair began to grow again,
as the Philistines continued to make of him great sport.
One day, as they gathered in the house of Dagon their god;
in a drunken stupor, they began to retort,
"Our god has delivered Samson into our hand!"
He will trouble us no more!"
"for his God has forsaken him,
and he will never be as before!"

So they set him between two pillars of the house.
And Samson said as he hung his head,
"O Lord God, Remember me. I pray,
let your strength return to me;
that I may be avenged of these Philistines this day."

He bowed his head, and relied once more on the Lord's might.
He pushed on the pillars, and the building collapsed.
Great was the slaughter of the Philistines,
and awesome was the sight!
So Samson died, along with those in the house;
And although the choices he made, brought him great strife;
those that he slew in his death

were more than he slew his entire life!

Now there is a lesson to be learned.
"How can a man take fire into his bosom,
and his clothes not be burned?"
We are not to consort with the enemy;
but we are to resist him, and give him no place.
We must attend to God's wisdom,
and lean on the keeping power of God's grace.
For the commandment of the Lord is a lamp,
and his law is light.
Let us heed his reproofs and instructions;
For they will be to the heart a great rejoicing,
and to the soul a delight!

DAVID
"A MAN AFTER GOD'S OWN HEART"

...for the Lord sees not as a man sees;
for man looks on the outward appearance,
but the Lord looks on the heart.
1 Samuel 16.7

The Lord spoke to the prophet Samuel,
so many years ago,
"Fill your horn with oil, and go to the house of Jesse,
and there I will cause you to know;
that the king I have provided for Israel
will be found among his sons.
For there will be in Jesse's house
my chosen, anointed one."

Now Samuel did as the Lord had spoken,
and took his journey to Bethlehem.
And there he found Jesse's seven sons
all who looked able, fit, and trim.

When Eliab, Jesse's eldest,
stood before Samuel on that day,
the prophet thought he met the requirements
of a king in every way.
The Lord then said unto Samuel,
"Judge not according to his countenance;
my anointing do not impart;
judge not by the height of his stature;
for I look upon the heart."

Then Jesse called for his sons,
Abinadab and Shammah and the other four.
"Is the king found among these"?
the father did implore.
Samuel said to Jesse,
"Tell me one thing please.
Do you have anymore children?
For the king is not among these"!

In amazement Jesse declared,
"There is one named David, who is the keeper of the sheep,
and the youngest of them all;

not at all like his brothers;
not as strong or tall."
Samuel said unto Jesse,
"Send and fetch him unto me.
For I will not sit down and rest
until this lad I am able to see!"

Now this lad did not look strapping or strong.
Although he had a beautiful countenance,
everything else about him looked wrong!
But as he stood before the prophet of God,
the Lord erased all of Samuel's doubt.
For the Lord knew David's love and devotion to him,
and that's what it's all about!
God said unto Samuel,
"Arise and anoint, for this is he."
And Samuel knew it was exactly
the way God wanted it to be.

Now we may look or feel inadequate
to accomplish our God-given part.
And there are those who may judge us outwardly,
but the Lord truly knows our heart.
The purpose he has placed in us,
is not according to our own ability.
But God is looking for our love and devotion,
so he can make us what he wants us to be.

Jehoshaphat
"Stand Still And See The Salvation Of The Lord"

There came a time
when the Ammonites and Moabites
came up to battle
against Jehoshaphat, Judah's king,
and a tremendous fear and trembling,
the enemy did bring.

There came some to Jehoshaphat declaring,
"Great is the multitude that is coming,
from beyond the sea;
an innumerable host of mighty men,
far mightier than we could ever be."

Jehoshaphat feared when he heard the news,
so he set himself to seek the Lord,
instead of singing the blues.
He called for Judah to gather,
and proclaimed a solemn fast throughout the land.
Jehoshaphat knew that the victory would come,
only according to God's divine plan.

Jehoshaphat stood in the house of the Lord,
and began to pray;
"O, God of our fathers, are you not the great God of heaven,
and do you not still rule over kingdoms today?
And in your hand, is there not power and might,
so that none is able to withstand?
Are you not our faithful God,
who drove out the inhabitants of the land?
And did you not give it to the seed of Abraham,
the very one whom you called friend;
With this land you blessed your people, Israel,
to give them an inheritance without end."

"We have built you this house,
and herein is your great name.

We know you are the God of heaven and earth.
You will always remain the same.
And now O God, against this great army,
we certainly have no might,
But we know this great and mighty company
is nothing in your sight"!
And Lord, we can't say we understand,
but this one thing we'll do;
we'll trust with all our hearts,
and keep our eyes on you"!
As all of Judah stood before the Lord,
they reverently and patiently waited.
And soon came the Spirit, into the congregation;
for the word of the Lord is never belated.

Then Jahaziel, under the unction of the Spirit, declared,
"hearken, Jerusalem and Judah, to all God has to say.
By reason of this great multitude,
be not afraid nor dismayed.
Keep your eyes on him,
and he will show you the way.
Tomorrow you will go down against them,
But you are to set yourselves and be still,
All you are required to do,
is to watch him unfold his perfect will.
For the battle is not yours;
this is not your fight.
For you shall see the salvation of the Lord,
and it will be awesome in your sight"!

Jehoshaphat bowed his head,
with his face to the ground.
Among all the inhabitants,
there arose a worshipful sound.
All the children of the tribe of Levi,
lifted their voices on high.

For Judah and Jerusalem knew their God was nigh.
They rose up early in the morning,
and went to the wilderness of Tekoa,
a dry and barren place.
But they went forth in the confidence
of God's amazing grace.
Jehoshaphat cried,
"Trust now in our mighty God;
on his word you must believe.
Believe also in his prophets,
and from his hand you shall receive."
When he had thus spoken,
he appointed singers to lead the way.
They went forth praising the beauty of his holiness;
and thanking him for the grace and mercy to face the day.

When the enemy heard the sound of worship,
the great multitude turned against itself.
They began to utterly destroy each other,
until not one alive was left.

When Jehoshaphat and all the people,
came to take the spoil away,
there were riches and precious jewels in abundance;
to gather it all, it took three days.

They assembled in the Valley of Berachah,
on the fourth day.
They blessed the Lord, and thanked him,
for the victory he had brought their way.
Then they returned again unto Jerusalem;
with a great celebration, they did rejoice.
For they were so very glad,
they had made the Lord their choice.

Now praise and worship is the key to victory,

in our heated battles.
Also do not allow the enemy any place,
or he your faith will rattle.
Even when it seems as though
you are facing overwhelming odds,
just remember the battle is not yours;
it belongs to God.
You can say along with Jehoshaphat,
as did all of Judah and Jerusalem;
"I will trust in the Lord with all my heart,
and keep my eyes on him!"
For every promise of God in Christ,
is yea and amen.
And you will find his promises to be true,
time and time again!

Nehemiah

So the wall was finished
in the twenty and fifth day of the month Elul, in fifty and two days.
And it came to pass, that when all our enemies heard thereof,
and all the heathen that were about us saw these things;
they were much cast down in their own eyes;
for they perceived that this work was wrought of our God.
Nehemiah 6:15-16

In the ninth month of the twentieth year,
of King Artaxerxes' reign,
Nehemiah received some troubling news,
that changed his countenance and brought his heart pain.

For Hanani, Nehemiah's brother,
told of the devastating condition of their beloved Jerusalem.
Those escaped of the captivity,
were in great affliction and reproach;
and the probability for their survival seemed slim.
The walls of the city were broken down,
and the gates were burned with fire.
Jerusalem was once again exposed to her enemies;
her situation was extremely dire.

It came to pass that when Nehemiah
heard all the disturbing words,
he wept and mourned certain days.
And before the God of heaven and earth,
he fervently fasted and prayed;
"I beseech you, O great and terrible God.
You keep your covenant and mercy,
toward them who love you.
To those who keep your commandments,
you abide forever true".
"Let your ears be attentive and your eyes open,
that you may hear your servant's prayer.
For the children of Israel, I pray day and night,
for you are the God who cares!
I confess both my sins and the sins of my father.
To you, my all I sincerely relent.
Israel has been corrupt before you.
Now O God, I pray that they have a heart to repent."
"Attend to my words, O Lord.
Hear my prayer, for I choose to fear your name.
Let Jerusalem be revived from among the ashes,

that we no longer bring you shame.
Prosper your servant this day,
and grant me mercy in the sight of the king;
that I may go and rebuild the walls.
Now give me strength to do this thing."

Now Nehemiah was the cupbearer,
unto Artaxerxes, the king.
He had direct access, into the king's presence,
and much influence to petition him for anything.
So it came to pass on a certain day,
that Nehemiah was serving the king his wine.
Nehemiah's countenance was very sad,
and in his heart there were many disappointments,
that made him sorely repine.
How he longed to return to the holy city Jerusalem,
that once was the land of his forefathers' dreams.
But now it was burned, wasted, in ruins;
there was no hope for Jerusalem's future,
or so it surely seemed.

King Artaxerxes said,
"Nehemiah, why are you so sick of heart"
If there is anything I can do for you,
please let me know my part."
Nehemiah answered the king with a gratefulness:
"O king if it pleases you,
and if I have found favor in your sight,
Please, allow me to return to Jerusalem,
so that, with God's help, I can try to make everything right."

The king then questioned,
"How long shall be your journey,
and when shall you return"?
After Nehemiah gave him a set time,
the king said, "go with my approval,

and accomplish all that your heart yearns".

King Artaxerxes sent letters,
to the governors beyond the river,
and to Asaph, the keeper of the forest of the trees;
that Asaph would give to Nehemiah
all the timber that he pleased.
So an abundance of timber was given
for the gates of the palace and also for the walls.
The good hand of God was on Nehemiah,
so the work would not stall.

Sanballat, the Horonite,
and his servant Tobiah, the Ammonite,
heard that the great work on the city had begun;
they were exceedingly grieved that someone
had come to assist in the welfare of Israel;
so they purposed for Nehemiah's plan to be undone.
They laughed and scorned and despitefully said,
"What is this thing that you plan to do"?
"You have rebelled against the king!
This we know to be true!"
Nehemiah declared, "the God of heaven will prosper us,
in this thing we do!
You have no portion, nor right nor memorial, in Jerusalem
We will give no place to you"!

First Eliashib built the sheep gate;
he sanctified it and set up the doors.
Each new day brought a determination,
that was greater than the day before.
Each group of workers were given their duties,
and they eagerly did their part.
God strengthened their hands for each new task,
and with great joy he requited their hearts.

Sanballet and Tobiah returned again
with great indignation, to mock and scorn;
"What can you feeble Jews do"?
"Will you be able to fortify"?
"Will you be able to revive the stones
from the heaps of the rubbish"?
"On your God are you able to rely"?
"Will you faint before the end of the day"?
"Is your God truly concerned about you"?
"Does your God really hear you when you pray"?
"You'll never see this job through."

Nehemiah once again prayed,
"Hear O God, for we are despised;
turn their reproach upon their own heads!"
"Let not their sins be blotted out from before you.
We have done this great work as you have led."
Now half the wall was quickly built,
for the people had a mind to work.
When the enemies of Jerusalem,
heard that the work was successfully progressing,
they became wroth and went berserk!
After Nehemiah had made his prayer to God,
he set a watch against the enemy day and night.
Judah became fearful over all the adversaries threats.
Many voiced their negative opinions,
and offered nothing but discouraging regrets.
The enemy said, "Judah will not know nor be able to see,
until we come into the city to destroy,
and cause the work to cease."

This did not sway nor deter Nehemiah;
the defense on the wall he increased.
So from that time forth,
half of the men worked on the wall,
the other half handled shields and spears.

And Nehemiah was faithful to remind them,
that God was with them and they had nothing to fear.
So many continued on in the building of the wall.
The rest held their shields and spears;
and faithfully watched from the rising of the morning,
until the night stars appeared.

Now the wall was finally finished;
it took only fifty-two days.
The enemy had tried, but failed, to hinder the work;
for Nehemiah trusted in all God's ways.

Now there are times when God may put
our hands to a needed task.
Let us have a ready mind to work,
and joyfully do all he asks.
Do not focus on the discouragements,
the enemy will try to bring.
Just simply trust God for the necessary strength,
and praise him in all things.

ELIJAH
"HOW LONG WILL YOU HALT BETWEEN TWO OPINIONS"?

So Ahab sent word throughout all Israel and assembled
the prophets on Mount Carmel.
Elijah went before the people and said,
"How long will you halt between two opinions"?
"If the Lord is God, follow him, but if Baal is God, follow him."
And the people answered him not a word.
1 Kings 18.20-21

In the thirty-eighth year of Asa, king of Judah,
an evil king began to reign over Israel;
Ahab was his name.
And he reigned for twenty-two years,
and brought upon the land a great shame.

He did evil, in the eyes of the Lord,
more than all other kings before.
He led God's people into gross sins;
and this, God greatly abhorred.

He married the daughter of the king of the Zidonians.
She was the wicked Jezebel.
Ahab considered it a trivial thing,
to disregard the God of heaven, and against him rebel.
So in Samaria, Ahab built many altars,
and a massive temple to the false deity, Baal.
The true God of Israel was soon forgotten,
as idol worship and sacrifice prevailed.

Now a time of reckoning came to Israel,
from God's own hand.
For three and one half years, God shut up the heavens,
and a severe drought covered the land.
God sent his prophet Elijah, to warn king, Ahab,
just how dire the circumstances would be.
And before this plight was over,
the power of the true living God, Ahab would see.

Toward the end of the long drought,
God told Elijah, "return to Samaria,
and speak unto Ahab, and do not refrain.
Tell him on the thirsty, parched land,
I am going to send an abundance of rain."
Ahab and the governor of his house, Obadiah,
went out looking for grass and water,

to feed the horses and other beasts.
On the road outside the city,
Obadiah and Elijah meet.
Elijah said unto Obadiah,
"Ahab is the one I need to see
"Tell him Elijah is here,
so please go and fetch him for me.".

When Ahab saw Elijah, he began to quickly retort,
"You are he who troubles all the land"!
Elijah replied, "It is not me but you"!
"You have forsaken God's commands."
"Go now and gather all of Israel together.
Unto Mount Carmel, you are to bring,
the four hundred fifty prophets of Baal.
Do not fail to do this thing!"
"Also bring the four hundred prophets of the groves,
who at Jezebel's table lavishly feast."
Now Ahab, Jezebel, and all their prophets,
didn't seem to be worried in the least.

So Ahab sent unto all the children of Israel,
and gathered the prophets together in the mount.
The multitude came from all directions,
and when they arrived they were too innumerable to count.

Elijah came to all the people,
who had gathered there.
They would witness a mighty manifestation of the Lord
of which they were totally unaware!
Elijah challenged the people,
"How long will you halt between two opinions?
If God be the true living God,
then him you must serve!
To trust in something of stone or wood,
you really have the nerve!"

God had proved himself to them so many times,
yet away from him they turned.
In spite of God's mighty miracles,
it seemed as though they would never learn.
Elijah continued, "If Baal be God,
then by all means, follow him"!
The true God would soon be revealed,
and for the other, his credential,
was looking awfully slim.

Elijah said,
"We will slay two bullocks, and cut them in pieces,
Let the prophets of Baal place one bullock,
on the altar they prepare.
I will dress the other bullock,
and place it on the altar of my God over there.
Now Baal's prophets are not to put
a fire upon their altar,
and rest assured, neither will I!
Call upon the name of your gods,
and to them fervently cry!
And the God that answers by fire,
we will serve him and on him diligently rely."

Now the prophets of Baal called upon their god,
from morning until noon.
They knew that they would faint,
if Baal did not answer soon.
When it began to look hopeless,
more drastic measures they took
Elijah just stood and mocked them,
and gave them a disbelieving look.
Elijah said, "Cry a little louder,
your god may be on a journey or just asleep!"
But from their god, they didn't hear a peep.
Then they began to cut themselves,

as Baal worshippers would often do.
Elijah said, "cry aloud as long as you want,
but your dead god will never answer you!"

With confidence, Elijah proceeded to build
the altar of the Lord.
For he knew he would receive an answer,
when Jehovah God he implored.
So Elijah took twelve stones,
one for each of Israel's tribes.
He knew that his God,
would not have to be coaxed or even bribed.

Elijah made a trench around the altar,
and laid the sacrifice on the wood.
he called for four barrels of water,
and began to soak it down the best he could.
He then called for eight more barrels of water,
to be poured on the altar round about.
All who were watching began to wonder what he was doing;
some even had a lot of serious doubts.
Now everything pertaining to the altar was thoroughly drenched.
There was even water overflowing from the trench.

And it came to pass at the time of the offering
of the evening sacrifice,
that Elijah began to pray:
"O, Lord God of Abraham, Issac and Jacob,
let it be known today,
that I am your servant,
and I have done all these things at your word,
and in your way."
After praying all his prayer,
there was excitement in the air;
For the fire of God fell;
and not only consumed the sacrifice,

but the wood and stones as well.
The fire also licked up the water in the trench.
The power of the Spirit left the false prophets bewildered,
the hearts of the people wrenched.

There was not one who could remain standing,
but all fell on their face.
And God's people again realized that his judgment
was wrapped in his mercy and unfailing grace.

Then Elijah knew all the false prophets
had to be slain;
for along with Ahab and Jezebel,
they had caused Israel great pain.
So they were taken down to the brook of Kishon,
there they all lost their lives.
Elijah was glad that never again,
with those false prophets would he have to strive!
Elijah told Ahab,
"Get up, eat and drink,
for I hear the sound of abundance of rain."
Ahab went to eat and drink,
and Elijah went to pray.
He climbed to the top of Mount Carmel;
so with God to get away.
He put his face between his knees,
and told his servant to go
and look toward the sea.
The servant returned saying "I saw nothing"
So Elijah sent him back seven times.
Now the servant knew if he could just see something,
it would truly be sublime!

And sure enough, the last time he went,
he was awe-struck and amazed;
for a cloud the size of a man's hand,

in the heavens was raised!
Elijah told his servant to go give Ahab the news.
Meanwhile the skies darkened
and a great wind blew.
In the rain, Ahab rode his chariot
toward the city gates.
The hand of the Lord was on Elijah,
and he girded his loins and outran the chariot,
and sat down in the city to wait.

"GOD DELIVERS AGAIN"

Shadrach, Meshach, and Abednego,
answered and said to the king,
"O, Nebuchadnezzar, …
If it be so, our God whom we serve,
is able to deliver us from the burning fiery furnace,
and he will deliver us out of your hand, O king"!
Daniel 3:16-17

When Shadrach, Meshach, and Abednego
would not bow to the king's idols of gold;
the angered king said to the three,
who were most determined and bold;
"Now at the sound of the music,
my command you are to heed"!
"You'll be thrown into the fiery furnace;
if you don't bow, and worship my gods indeed"!

Then said the three,
"Only to the one true living God, will we bow!
To start the music, there's no need"!
The king boasted, "Who is your God,
that he can deliver you from me"?
Then said the three,
"He is the only God who IS ABLE to deliver!
"And he will deliver us, you'll see"!

The king exclaimed in frustration:
"Because you would not bow
to my idols made of gold,
Let's see if YOUR GOD will deliver,
as you have boldly stood here and told."!

Now the three Hebrew children
didn't know how God would work things out,
but they knew they had to keep on believing,
and give no place to doubt!

So the king summoned his mighty men
and handed them down a decree;
"I'll teach those foolish Hebrews.
They'll wish they would have bowed their knees.!
Turn on my fiery furnace, seven times hotter than before;
and bind them about their hands and feet,
with strong, unbreakable cords!

These three have troubled my kingdom
and have brought great discord;
Quickly cast them into the flames,
so they will trouble me no more"!

Now the fiery furnace was made so hot,
just as the king had related,
that the mighty men, who threw them in,
were instantly cremated.

Now the king arose in amazement,
and called for all his wise men.
"Do we not agree that we threw in three,
so will you count for me again?
I see four pacing the floor,
and the forth is not as mortal men!"
Then the king declared in great astonishment
as all the court drew near.
"There must truly be something awesome
about this God whom they hold dear"!

Now Shadrach, Meshach, and Abednego
were brought forth from the midst of the fire.
Their hair was not singed, their bodies not burned,
nor was there even smoke on their attire!
The king then decreed,
"anyone who speaks anything against this God amiss,
will certainly meet with a terrible fate,
far greater than this"!
Then King Nebuchadnezzar boldly proclaimed,
"Blessed be the God of the Hebrew children three;
For he is the great God who delivers,
and he made a believer out of me!"

DANIEL
"A MAN OF GODLY INTEGRITY"

Now when Daniel knew that the writing was signed,
he went into his house; and his windows being opened
in his chamber toward Jerusalem, he kneeled upon his knees
three times a day, and prayed, and gave thanks before his God,
as he did aforetime.
Daniel 6.10

There once was a man named Daniel,
who had an excellent spirit indeed.
He worshipped only the Great God of Heaven,
and faithfully dedicated his life to a godly creed.
Now Darius was the King of the land called Babylon,
of which Daniel was part.
And King Darius knew that Daniel
loved his God with all his heart.

But not all within the kingdom tolerated Daniel's devotion;
There were those who wanted to entrap this man of God;
So they put a wicked scheme into motion.
All the presidents and princes began to petition the king;
"Make a royal law and establish a firm decree,
that for thirty days no man is allowed to ask of their God anything!
And if they do, they will be thrown into the lion's den;
Now O, king sign the decree and put your seal without and within".

Now these men knew right well how faithful Daniel was to pray.
They knew he bowed on his knees with his face toward Jerusalem,
gave thanks and worshipped three times a day.
When Daniel heard that a decree had been signed, sealed and sent,
his faith did not waver, he kept on praying and refused to relent!

Then the schemers assembled and found Daniel praying,
just as he had faithfully done oftentimes before.
So they went immediately to the King and declared,
"This Law of the Medes and Persians cannot be altered or ignored"!
Now the king quickly realized,
that he had been made a part of a deadly plot,
so he set his heart to deliver Daniel,
because he knew his excellent character had no blemish or blot.

But the schemers repeatedly pressed on the king,
that the law of the land could not be changed.
It had to be carried out to the fullest,

and could not be rearranged!
So the king had no choice,
but to cast Daniel into the lion's den.
But Daniel knew that his God
was able to deliver time and time again!

Now the king returned to his palace
to spend a sleepless night;
but arose in haste in the morning,
to check on Daniel at first light.
With a loud voice the king lamented,
"O, Daniel, was your God able to deliver"?
"Yes, O king my God sent his angel,
and the lions' mouths were cemented"!
Now King Darius was exceedingly glad
about Daniel's joyful sound;
And when Daniel was brought up to stand before the king,
no manner of hurt on him was found!

Now the schemers were brought forth,
along with their children and wives;
and for their evil deed, they all lost their lives!
King Darius then declared,
"In every dominion of my kingdom,
Daniel's God is to be feared!
For HE is the true God of heaven and earth,
and greatly to be revered"!
So Daniel prospered in the reigns
of Darius and Cyrus, the kings.
And Daniel lived on to see
many wondrous things!

"Standing With The Patriarchs"

Wherefore seeing we also are compassed
about with so great a cloud of witnesses,
Let us lay aside every weight, and the sin
which doth so easily beset us,
and let us run with patience the race that is set before us,
Looking unto Jesus the author and finisher of our faith;
who for the joy that was set before him endured the cross,
despising the shame, and is set down
at the right hand of the throne of God.
Hebrews 12:1-2

Wouldn't it be very interesting
If those old Patriarchs of faith and grace,
Could come, sit and talk with us
in our meeting place?
Have you thought just what they might say?

What say you, Abraham?
What did you think
when you were called into a strange land?
Not having a clue as to where you were going;
what a leap of faith, not knowing all God's plan!
Furthermore, how did you keep on believing
when God asked you to give your son?
How could you do this,
knowing he was your most precious one?
How could you endure such an impossible test?
How were you able to trust him with your very best?

Oh, my fellow – believers,
God allowed me to see through the telescope of time;
to a place called Mt. Calvary,
to a sacrifice sublime!
What a beautiful glimpse into God's eternal plan!
What an unspeakable sacrifice given to mortal man!
So dear fellow – believers:
It is not about what I could do for him,
but what HE has done for you and me!!
For that sacrifice was God's provision
so you and I could live eternally!

What say you Job?
If you were that perfect man,
why did you suffer so many sore trials?
If you would have been the man you should have been,
none of this would have come on you, you see;
And God, being a God of mercy,

should have never allowed all this to be?
Why did you even try to serve the Lord,
and walk before him righteously?
When you were trying to shun evil
in a wicked and perverse land;
why would you even bother
when all you could see was God's angry hand?
Why didn't you take the advice of your nagging wife?,
'Curse God and Die!'
Don't you think it would have been
so much better than your troubled life?

Oh my dear fellow believers,
do not be as my nagging wife or so-called friends.
For God's infinite wisdom goes beyond
what man can comprehend!
Yes, God wanted to know what was truly in my heart!
Would I lose my godly integrity?
Would I fall apart?
May all who look upon me be able to clearly see;
although I did not have answers for everything,
I had to simply trust, for he knew what was best for me!

What say you, Daniel?
The decree had already been signed!
Did you hopelessly return to your house,
close your shutters, draw your curtains, and pine?

No, fellow believers, I'm proud to tell you today,
I ran all the way home and went into my secret place to pray.
There I turned my thoughts and face homeward, to old Jerusalem.
I fell on my knees and cried to God;
knowing that I could always trust in him!
O yes, I was still thrown into the Lion's den;
but those lions had lost their appetite.
Don't you know dear fellow believers,

that even in the Lion's den, God can still make everything right?

What say you, Jeremiah?
How many times were you told
to forever cease from your prophesying?;
Yet you continued to be bold!
Yes, we all know that the word of God
was as a fire shut up in your bones;
but if you would have kept on with that preaching,
you might have found yourself standing alone!

Well, dear fellow believers, that is quite alright.
For the chief governor imprisoned me,
and fastened me in those prison stocks tight.
Oh yes, that chief governor just wanted to humiliate;
Oh, but even in the prison house, the word of God is great!

What say you little David?
What good were those stones and sling?
Up against Goliath, you looked like a puny little thing.
The situation was hopeless!
The best you could have done was retreat.
For this mighty giant would easily defeat!

Oh, fellow believers, why do you look at his size?
There is nothing too hard for God;
don't you realize?
To fear and doubt you must never yield!
For God is ever faithful to be your shield!
That old giant came against me with spear and sword!
I came against him in the name of the Lord!

What say you Stephen?
A Spirit-filled man of faith, power and wisdom;
doing miracles throughout the land.
What was the purpose of your faithfulness;
just to fall into deceitful hands?

Oh dear fellow believers,
I served the Lord diligently and this I did by choice!
The Holy Spirit had an eternal purpose
for giving me a bold voice!
For the word of God increased, the gospel trail was laid;
And up against eternity, my life was a small price paid!

What say you, Moses?
What made you leave Egypt's treasures
with all its worldly comforts, and alluring pleasures?
Why would you choose to give up the palace
for the sting of the taskmaster's whip?
You must have been suffering from insanity;
You needed to get a grip!
Why would you choose the mud pits,
living the life of a slave?
Surely, this is the way only a madman would behave!

Oh my fellow-believers
I cannot explain all God allowed my faith to see;
It was not in the splendor of Egypt,
but the back side of the desert,
where God revealed himself to me!
Just one glimpse of his glory caused me to understand,
the purpose God had for me was far greater than grand!
It was in the parched wilderness,
where God etched his glory on my face;
And you can always find the same glory I found,
in your dry and barren place.

What say you, Joseph?
What good did it do you to dream?
For when you spoke it to your brothers,
they began to scheme!
Your dreams only brought you distress, turmoil
and every ungodly thing!

Oh my fellow believers,
I can tell you without a doubt;
God had a plan for me,
I had to let him work it out!
There's no way I could have ever known
what God was going to do!
So keep on dreaming and hoping;
For God is faithful and true!

Now, what say you, fellow – believers;
declared the old patriarchs of faith.
All our lives have testified of God's amazing grace.
We hope that as you look upon us as your examples,
you may stand faithful too.
We want you to know we are that great cloud of witnesses,
cheering just for you.
Lay aside the weights and sin that would so easily beset,
and run this race with patience, for you're not home quite yet!
You can look unto Jesus, the great author and finisher of your faith,
and know that you can make it by that same amazing grace.

"John The Baptist"

The voice of him that crieth in the wilderness,
"Prepare ye the way of the Lord."
Isaiah 40.3

Jesus, one day, boarded a ship,
to go into a desert place apart.
He had just received the news of his cousin John's death,
and this had pricked his heart.
Many were the people that came out of the cities,
to press on him along his way;
He was moved with great compassion
and healed much of the multitude that day.
It had not been long since John had sent his disciples to Jesus,
as he waited in his prison cell.
"Are you the one or do we look for another"
Jesus simply replied: "Go your way to John and tell;
the blind is seeing, the lame is walking,
the gospel is being preached;
the deaf is hearing, the leper is cleansed,
the poor is being reached."

Although John did not live to see
the fulfillment of salvation's plan,
He knew the purpose for Jesus' coming,
was far greater than he was able to understand!
For blind were the sinners, they could not see,
for sin had darkened their hearts;
without hope were the lame, they could not trod
the righteous paths of God
The souls of men were leprous, so defiled by sin;
They would not hear the voice of God,
speaking to their conscience within,
But the Dayspring of Hope was coming up behind
the one who was "preparing the way"
To give light to them in darkness,
to usher in the dawning of a brand new day.
To make a highway of holiness,
that mankind may walk on and not stray;
To cleanse the leprous marks of sin

from off the the souls of men,
that the sinner might give heed to his conscience,
speaking from deep within.

Now John was a simple man,
with a diet of locust and honey,
and camel's hair for his attire;
baptizing with water for remission of sin,
preaching of one who would baptize with Holy Ghost and fire.

John walked a sober and mortified life.
He was not as a reed in the wind,
bending beneath every temptation and strife.
Oh, that we might learn from him;
that this also is the way we must be.
We must have a steady, made up mind;
not being tossed, as the wave of the sea.

Now Jesus bestowed a great memorial on John,
as he made this honorable decree;
"Among those that are born of women,
there's no greater prophet than he."

And now everyone in the Kingdom of God
has been given endless opportunities;
to stand unashamed like John, and boldly declare
the blessings of the Gospel of Peace.

"As a Little Child"

And Jesus called a little child unto him,
and set him in the midst of them, and said,
'Verily, I say unto you, except you be converted,
and become as little children, you shall not enter into
the kingdom of heaven.
Whosoever therefore shall humble himself as a little child,
the same is greatest in the kingdom of heaven.
Matt. 18.2-4

Oftentimes, great multitudes followed Jesus,
as he taught along the shores of Galilee;
Pressing on him to touch the lame,
heal the deaf, and make the blinded eyes to see.
It was his joy to reach out to others,
to make a difference along the way;
even as he delights to bless his people
who fully trust in him today.

Jesus was always moved with compassion,
on those who came seeking with a pureness of heart.
For many came in faith believing,
and on these, his healing mercies he did impart.
But not all came seeking with honest intentions.
Some came tempting him in all he would say;
such as the Sadducees and Pharisees,
the self-righteous ones of that day.
These groups did not thirst for knowledge of the truth;
they judged according the Law of Moses quite well;
They just wanted to entrap Jesus in his teachings,
then run to the synagogue to tell.
They carefully watched to accuse him,
of ministering against the law;
And they were eager to misinterpret,
any miracles they saw.

So it must have been a welcomed sight,
when little children, to Jesus, drew near.
The simple faith and of these little ones,
our Lord so greatly endeared.
He had dealt with the proud religious crowd,
with their pomp and pious sway;
but now he would teach about his Father's Kingdom,
using the little children who were about him that day.

A way called Holiness,

for us has been prepared.
And we must be born again,
just as Jesus declared.
The only way to enter the gates of that city,
is to be converted and become as a little child;
Not having a mind for evil or malice,
but a heart that is humble and mild.

Now the secret to the kingdom of Heaven
will open up when we begin to see,
that the greatest found among us,
will as a little child be.
We must not be as the pomp and pious;
For the Word of God has clearly shown,
that we stand complete in the righteousness of Christ;
For we have no righteousness of our own.

"At The Feet Of One Another"

For I have given you an example,
that you should do as I have done to you.
John 13.15

One evening after supper,
as the Passover drew near;
Jesus began to teach his disciples,
whom he loved so dear.
Jesus arose and laid aside his garment,
as he had done once before;
when he set aside his heavenly garments,
to walk through humanity's door.
For the reason he came down to man
was not to be served, but to serve,
and to give his life a ransom for many;
the greatest gift so undeserved!
Jesus knew this lesson on "service and humility"
had to be taught by example, and not just word;
So Jesus poured a basin of water,
and a towel around him, he did gird.
Our Lord humbled himself and became a servant,
to wash his disciples' feet.
No greater example of humility,
No greater love, so sweet!
Jesus gave us this example,
that we should do as he has done.
We are to live a life of humble service,
until our race is successfully run.

At the feet of one another,
true humility starts.
At the feet of one another,
we hear the Lord's heart.
At the feet of one another,
we learn how love abounds.
At the feet of one another,
true forgiveness is found.
At the feet of one another,
we begin to understand,

that we are to one another,
God's extended hand.

For the greatest among us shall be servant;
The self-indulged shall be abased;
But the one with a heart for others,
will be exalted by HIS amazing grace.
Yes, we call Jesus Master and Lord,
and this we say quite well.
But how we humbly serve one another,
is the true test that will always tell.

"The Upper Room"

And suddenly there came a sound from heaven
as of a rushing mighty wind, and it filled all the house where
they were sitting.
And there appeared unto them cloven tongues like as of fire,
and it sat upon each of them.
And they were all filled with the Holy Ghost,
and began to speak with other tongues,
as the Spirit gave the utterance.
Acts 2.2-4

After Jesus Christ arose,
he was seen of his disciples and others,
for the length of forty days.
He spoke of things pertaining to the kingdom of God,
and proved to them his resurrection in many infallible ways.

Before he ascended, he left them a command;
that they should tarry at Jerusalem,
for the promise of the Father,
which was a part of the fullness of God's plan.
Jesus said, "John truly baptized with water,
for the remission of sin,
but you shall be baptized
with the Holy Ghost within."

Jesus continued on to explain,
"You shall be a witness unto me,
in Jerusalem, Judea, and Samaria
and the uttermost part of the earth."
And through the outpouring of the Spirit,
many would come to know the new birth.
For the bold witness the disciples would receive,
would lead countless others to believe.

So when he had spoken these things to his disciples,
while they beheld, a cloud received him out of their sight.
And behold two men stood by them,
dressed in garments of pure white.
These two gave to them an assurance,
that we hold dear even today;
The blessed assurance of his return,
on God's appointed day.

So the disciples took their Sabbath day's journey,
back to Jerusalem, from the mountain of Olivet.
They were filled with wonder,

although they could not understand all things quite yet.
When they arrived back into Jerusalem,
they went into an upper room.
They were probably like many of us today;
they had God's plan figured out, or so they presumed!

Jesus had spoken of the time,
when his disciples would endure many hard things.
They would be beaten, and imprisoned;
They would be delivered up before governors and kings.
They would stand before councils,
to give a fervid testimony of him.
They would be hated for his name's sake,
and their sufferings would be grim.
But he reassured them when they were delivered up,
they would know what to speak in that selfsame hour.
The effectual witnesses they would become
would be through the demonstration of Holy Ghost power.
It would be this power that would enable them to withstand,
the onslaught of persecution,
and give them grace to fulfill God's foreordained plan.

On the day of Pentecost,
they were with one accord, in prayer and supplication,
as they waited to see all God would do.
Suddenly, there came a sound from heaven,
and they realized God's promise to them was true!
For the sound was as of a rushing mighty wind,
and it filled all the house where they sat.
What they were about to see and experience,
they would never forget!

And there appeared unto them
cloven tongues like as of fire,
Now, not just some were filled with the Holy Ghost,
but the whole house, entire!

Many nations were represented in the city,
because of the Feast of Weeks.
They began to hear these Galileans,
in their native tongues speak.
Now as this was noised abroad,
the multitudes gathered about;
some in total amazement,
some in dispute and doubt.

Those in amazement said, "what does all this mean?"
For this was something unusual, that they had never seen.
The doubters shouted, "these men are full of new wine!"
For to them it seemed that these had become intoxicated,
and had gotten seriously out of line.!

But Peter, standing up with the eleven,
lifted up his voice that day;
"You men of Jerusalem and Judea,
hearken to what I have to say;
These men are not drunk as you suppose,
seeing it is but the third hour!
But this is that which was spoken by the prophet, Joel;
the Spirit would be poured out with glory and great power"!

Christ is exalted to the Father's right hand,
and he ever lives to intercede.
The earnest of the Spirit is in our hearts.
What more do we need?

Paul and Silas
"The Jailhouse Rocked"

And suddenly there was a great earthquake,
so that the foundations of the prison were shaken,
and immediately all the doors were opened,
and everyone's bands were loosed.
Act 16.26

As Paul and Silas were called by the Spirit into Macedonia,
into one of the chief cities called Philippi;
they did not know the full purpose for being there.
Except for the night vision given to Paul of a man's urgent cry.
"Come over into Macedonia and help us" was his plea;
so with assurance they knew that the Lord had called them,
and had ordained in them a mandated decree.

After abiding in the city certain days,
Paul and Silas went out of the city to a riverside,
where a women's prayer meeting was under way.
There was a woman there by the name of Lydia,
who was a seller of purple dye.
She eagerly heard the words spoken by Paul,
for salvation was her heart's cry.
Now the conviction of the Holy Spirit was so bold,
that not only was Lydia saved and baptized,
but also her entire household!

As Paul and Silas continued daily praying,
they were met by a damsel with a spirit of divination;
who brought her masters much gain by soothsaying.
She repeatedly followed after them crying,
"These men are the servants of the most high God,
which show us the way of salvation"
This she did for many days,
and brought Paul much grief and frustration.
He then turned and said to the spirit with Holy Ghost power,
"I command you in the name of Jesus Christ to come out of her!"
and he came out that selfsame hour!

Now her masters then saw and understood,
that the hope of their gains were gone;
So into the marketplace before the magistrates and rulers,
Paul and Silas were drawn.
The multitude rose up against them

"These men do trouble our city
and teach customs that we do not believe."
They are customs that are unlawful,
and being Romans, we cannot receive"!
So the magistrates commanded that they be beaten
and fastened in the stocks;
so after many stripes were placed on them,
they were thrown into the inner prison block.

Now the jailer was charged with the responsibility
of keeping them securely bound;
but at the midnight hour
he began hearing joyful sounds.
For Paul and Silas began singing and praising God,
and that's all it took.
For suddenly there was a great earthquake,
and the foundation of the prison shook!
Immediately the prison doors were opened,
and from the stocks, they were freed.
Paul and Silas knew that praise and worship
would bring them through any kind of need.
The keeper, waking from his sleep,
was quickened by an awful dread;
and seeing the prison doors opened,
he feared that all the prisoners had fled;

The keeper of the prison drew out his sword,
to do himself great bodily harm.
Then Paul cried with a loud voice saying,
"We are all here, do not be alarmed."
Then the keeper called for a light,
and sprang into the prison cell.
Fearfully shaking and trembling,
at the feet of Paul and Silas he fell.
And although he could not comprehend,
what all the commotion was about,

he knew enough to be convinced
these two served an awesome God, no doubt!

Then said the keeper, "I want this great gift of salvation";
"so how may I receive"?
Paul and Silas said, "salvation is for you and your house;
On the Lord Jesus Christ you must believe"!
So Paul and Silas shared the word of the Lord
and the keeper and all his house were baptized.
And although Paul and Silas had suffered persecution,
the plan God had for them in Phillipi was quickly realized.

"God's Great Creation"

I will praise you;
for I am fearfully and wonderfully made,
marvelous are your works;…..
Psalm 139.14

God created all by the power of his might,
He uttered out of darkness,
and commanded forth the light.
Everything he made, he declared it good;
and on all, he put his eternal ordinance,
so it would accomplish what it should.
For he spoke only once,
to the waters along the shore,
that they could rush inland,
only so far and no more.
When he created the Sparrow,
he gave him a song to sing;
and that little bird, at any time,
will let his praises ring.
The sun always knows
just when and where to brightly shine;
and the moon always knows how to perfectly align.
The fruit bearing trees are not confused,
on what they are to yield.
The stalk of corn also knows
how to grow up in the field.
The seasons seem to always come,
in their perfect time;
they accomplish what they are supposed to,
with a majestic glory, that is sublime!
The great starry constellations,
know their rightful place.
The lily of the valley
grows with the greatest poise and grace.
the beast of the forest knows how to hunt for prey;
and every creature great and small,
knows how to find food sufficient for the day.
The mighty and lofty eagle
knows it was created to soar on high;
and the mother eagle always knows

when to teach her young to fly.
Even the stubborn mountain goats
know their distinguishing traits,
and to all their young,
they simply know how to relate.
The winds know when to blow with a fury,
and they know when to just be still.
They have no problem at all,
moving according to the Great Creator's will.
And doesn't the Bible teach us,
we are to consider the little ant.
They scurry and scamper in a scanty rush,
through yards, over flowers and plants.
They are only doing what they were created to do.
Oh, mankind could learn from them quite well.
Although they seem insignificant,
they have a story to tell.
Yes, it is quite amazing how God's creation,
simply knows what to do;
but the greatest of all creation,
doesn't seem to have a clue.
Mankind was created for the Heavenly Father's glory and praise.
But we act as though we have no purpose,
in filling all our days.
But nevertheless, we were made
to know our ultimate goal;
It is to worship and serve our Great Creator,
with all our heart, spirit and soul.

"If We Could Have Lived Back Then"

There are those living today,
who think it would have been so grand;
If they could have placed their footprints
alongside the Lord's in the hot and burning sand.
If only I could have walked with him, they say,
by the shores of Galilee.
If only I could have been with him,
as he healed the sick,
and made the blinded eyes to see!
If only I could have been able
to sit and feast with him;
Oh just to watch him break the bread!
Or maybe I could have been
one of the thousands on the hillside,
that he so graciously fed!
Some say that it would have been so great,
to be standing by the tomb;
when Jesus commanded Lazarus to come forth,
from that cold and darkened room.
Many say they would have loved to be
in Peter's boat that night;
when Jesus arose and calmed the troubled sea,
as the fishermen trembled in fright!
Could you even imagine being with the Lord
as was Peter, James, and John;
when his glory shone before them,
on the Mountain of Transfiguration?
His face did shine as the sun.
His raiment was white as the light.
And when Moses and Elijah showed up,
it must have been a sight!
Many say they would have loved to walk
the cobblestone streets of old Jerusalem.
Many would have loved to see the woman healed
of the issue of blood;

just by touching his garment's hem.
I suppose if I could have lived back then
I would have loved to be,
with the Samaritan woman at the well;
when she heard and received the words of eternal life,
then ran back to the city to tell!
Or maybe I would have loved to be
with the two on the Emmaus way;
who said, "Did not our hearts burn within us,
as he opened the scripture to us today"?

But there is none of us so willing,
who would be able to readily say;
we would have liked to help him shoulder
the burden of the cross he bore that day!
Our Lord was the innocent, who died as guilty,
that we, the guilty, could live as free.
May we never forget the price he paid
that day at Calvary!

Now, it really doesn't matter,
the frame of time we've been granted to live.
But the greatest fulfillment of purpose,
is when our all to Jesus we give!

"Great Is God's Faithfulness"

Oh Lord, great is your faithfulness;
how true your covenant with Man!
I am told it is unto all generations,
the very surety to salvation's plan!
Oh Lord, great is your faithfulness;
how true your covenant with man!
It is as your eternal ordinance,
that established both night and day;
and just as they come with each season,
they do not pass away.

Oh Lord, great is your faithfulness;
how true is your covenant with man!
You stripped yourself of your deity,
to come and walk with man.
You took not on you the nature of angels,
but the seed of Abraham.
For as we are partakers of flesh and blood,
you like wise took part of the same;
to give us a hope that is steadfast;
to make us children, called by your name.

Oh Lord, I'm in awe of your faithfulness,
as I ponder your covenant with man.
When I consider the heavens,
and all the works of your hands;

who am I that you would be so faithful?
Why are you so mindful of man?
Your ways are past finding out!
Your faithfulness, too vast to understand!

"A Postcard From Heaven"

I dreamed I received a postcard;
and as I looked at it with amazement,
a smile came across my face.
The return address was marked Heaven,
that grand and glorious place.
I thought to myself,
"Who could be writing me from Heaven"?
"I know so many who are there."
And as I looked at the picture,
it was beautiful beyond compare!
There was a banquet table,
with what looked like golden chairs.
Plates and goblets and utensils
carved in intricate beauty, so rare!
The length of the table was endless
It seemed to go further than the eye can see!
I thought could this be the table being set
to usher in eternity?
On the other side of the postcard
was a little note which read,
"Blessed are they which are called
to the Marriage Supper of the Lamb;
being lovingly prepared by the great "I Am".
There is a great excitement on all who are here,
because they know the eternal celebration is near."
There will be untold gladness!

Every tongue will sing,
praises and honor to Jesus, our King"!
As I stood there weeping with postcard in hand,
my heart began longing for that home place so grand!
And as I looked upward, I felt a heavenly wind;
For I knew what my spirit anticipated most in life
was right around the bend!

"Lord, Teach Us To Pray"

Our Father, which art in heaven,
Hallowed be thy name.
Holy is your name, O Lord;
How magnificent throughout the earth!
There's no other name under heaven,
whereby we may experience the new birth!
For that name that is above all names
is eternally the same,
Yesterday, Today and Forever;
steadfast and glorious is this name!
Blessed be the name of the Lord!
Let all his creation sing;
for HE and HE alone
has done many wondrous things!

Thy kingdom come.
Your kingdom is an everlasting kingdom,
ever increasing and without an end;
established in all your children,
who by faith have been born again!
The kingdom of righteousness, peace and joy
is not from without, but within.
The temporal things of earth shall be shaken,
so that the eternal may remain.
And the unshakable kingdom that God is preparing
we, by his grace will gain.

Thy will be done in earth,
as it is in heaven.
Lord, I am only an earthen vessel,
you fashioned out of clay.
But may this vessel be one of honor,
giving glory to you always.
As I humbly and prayerfully seek your will,
may I fervently walk in it day by day.
As your word is forever established in heaven,
let it be established in this earthen vessel, I pray.

Give us this day our daily bread.
Lord, you are the living bread from heaven.
Rain down on me always.
I do not ask for abundance,
but only that which is sufficient for the day.
You've been faithful in your providence;
you've provided for me in every way.
By your loving hand, I am fed.
Lord, give me evermore, that daily bread,
as I continue to trust in you.

And Forgive us our debts
Lord, I fear to think where I would be
if you had never died on Calvary's cross.
For I owed a debt that I could not pay;
I would be forever lost!
But I've been redeemed,
not by corruptible things;
such as silver and gold;
but by the precious blood of that perfect lamb.
The sacrifice too great to be told!
O Lord, my Savior, you knew no sin,
but was made to be sin for me.
This you did that I could know peace, and live eternally!
There is therefore now no condemnation

to all who will trust and believe.
And I only need to rest in you;
for I am assured your forgiveness I've received.
My heart is filled with gratitude.
It's my desire to live for you day by day.
May my life be a living sacrifice and testimony,
and pleasing to you, Lord, in every way!
Father, you are a great God of love and mercy;
and you loved me too much to excuse my sin.
Ever shine the light of your love,
and keep a check on my heart within.

As we forgive our debtors.
Who am I, Lord, if I say I cannot forgive
after being forgiven of so much?
How can I not reach out
to those who have offended me
after I've experienced your forgiving touch?
True forgiveness will open
the flood-gates of your love, O Lord,
and give me the peace of mind.
For just as I have known, Lord, that you are good
and graciously ready to forgive;
I have no excuse not to reach out to others,
so they can know your forgiveness and live.
May I never forget, but daily understand,
that I am to be, O Lord, your expression
in this lost and troublesome land.
Ever remind me, Lord, that I am your written epistle,
I am your extended hand.
When the world looks upon me, what will they see?
Will they see a forgiving heart?
May the fruit of the Holy Spirit be in me,
as forgiveness I choose to impart.

And lead us not into temptation,

There has no temptation taken me,
but such as is common to man.
But God you are faithful to strengthen me,
and enable me to stand.
Lord, you never promised
I would not have trials and cares;
but you reassured me that it would never be
more than I could bear.
Lord, you were driven into the wilderness
to be tempted by Satan's hand;
but the eternal Word of the Father
broke the devil's bands.
That same eternal Word of God
will also faithfully sustain me;
and give to me, as it did you Lord,
precious victory!
For the thoughts O Lord, you have towards me,
are for peace and not for evil,
to give me an expected end.
I can always trust and lean on you,
time and time again.

But deliver us from evil,
Deliver me from the evil one,
who is ever working to ensnare.
Keep me in your loving mercies,
and your tender care.
Lord, fill me with your perfect love;
so that I may victoriously win,
over all Satan's deadly devices,
and all this world's alluring sin.

**For thine is the kingdom, and the power,
and the glory, forever.**
Father, you are the Great Creator,
of everything I see.

On the balcony of nothing, you boasted your desire;
and caused all things to be.
All was brought forth by the strength of your word,
and the power of your might.
You uttered out of the darkness, and it became the light.
All things were made by you,
and without you nothing was made.
By your eternal ordinance,
the foundation of the earth was laid.
Father you are the beginning of all,
and at the end, all things will return to you.
You will ever reign with strength and salvation,
For your word is forever true.

Amen

"Love's Good News"

Many people rush to and fro,
searching for peace and love;
putting their trust in this world's instabilities,
instead of our Heavenly Father above.
Many have looked for "things" to hope in;
only to find the "things" insecure and frail.
Don't you think it's about time
to show a lost and dying world
our Jesus, who cannot fail?
Do you think we're doing enough
to get the good news told?
Let us not be slothful, timid, or ashamed,
but be diligent and bold!
For our Lord died for us all.
On Calvary, he took our place.
So may we live to faithfully show forth
his love, mercy and grace.
May we sanctify the Lord God in our hearts;
so we may be proud to share salvation's plan.
Let's be ready always to give a reason
of our hope to every man.
For all God's great and precious
promises in Christ
are not nay, but yea and amen!

"The Home Mama Built"

Mama built her home on love and faithfulness,
and raised her children therein.
What a strong, sturdy and enduring home,
this home has always been!

A home built on manifold wisdom;
where the law of kindness was near.
The lessons of life she taught me,
even today, resound in my ear.

A home not built on worldly riches,
but oftentimes on meager fare.
A home with a righteous foundation,
is truly a treasure beyond compare!

This home was not built without problems;
there were winds of adversity and pain;
but fortified within its walls,
was love's sweetest refrain!

There is something more precious than rubies,
and far more costly than gold;
it's the love of God shown through a mother;
the message too great to be told.

Mama built her home with a quiet resolution.
To her strength and honor, I can attest.
She has given to me a legacy,

that has become for me a quest.

The home that was built by Mama,
was a home at its very best!
She tended well to the ways of her household.
Her children arise and call her blessed.

Lovingly dedicated to Doris Kicklighter

I thank you, Mama, for your years of faithful dedication to your
children.

"A Letter To Papa"

Oftentimes I go in memory
to days of yesteryear.
Some days were sad and poignant;
but most were so precious and dear.
There is a day I hold so vividly,
and clear in my mind still today.
It's the day you took us on as your family.
Since then you've loved us
in your own caring way.
Papa, you never pushed your way into our hearts,
but one thing you did quite well;
you quietly and gently began to create
your own special place.
Now it's a space only you can fill.
You have been faithful so many years,
working alongside my mom;
to create a haven for my brother and me;
a place that we call home.
So Papa, I thank you for your tireless devotion,
and your unconditional love.
Our family has been blessed abundantly,
by our Heavenly Father above.
Love,
Leah

Lovingly dedicated to Eugene Kicklighter;
who went home to be with our Lord on August 20, 2007.

"More Than A Mother-In-Law"

You have been more than a Mother-In-Law;
you've been a kind and precious friend.
Always caring, sharing, and lending yourself;
this in you, I admire and commend.
There is a common bond that binds us;
it's the love for a husband and son.
For this reason we have joined
our two hearts as one.
I am truly a blessed woman.
Instead of one mom, I have two;
to inspire, teach, and encourage me;
as you so graciously do.
Please know that I'll always love this man,
who was once your little boy.
He is all the pride of life for me;
my happiness and my joy.

With Love and Respect,
Leah

Lovingly dedicated to Murial D. Ray
who went home to be with our Lord,
on February 24, 2012

"My Lifelong Friend"

God has blessed my life in many ways.
He has given me precious friends no doubt.
But there is one friend, who is so dear to me,
that I would like to tell you about.

This friend has been a part of my life,
since my earliest childhood days;
and has influenced my life,
in so many positive ways.

I have so many precious memories
of this lifelong friend.
To share all the fond memories in my heart,
I wouldn't know where to begin.
Of all my childhood memories,
some are better than the rest.
But the ones that include my lifelong friend,
I'll always remember as the very best!

When disappointments come my way,
as with everyone they do;
my lifelong friend always seems to know
how to chase away the blues.
My friend has been faithful to encourage me,
in my hopes and dreams.
And has always been quick to remind me,
the obstacles are never as big as they seem.

We have enjoyed many joyful times together,
and they have far outweighed the bad.
I can say without a doubt,
this friend is one of the best friends I've ever had!

My lifelong friend and I share a common bond,
that makes our friendship like no other;
we share the same Mom and Dad;
and I'm so very proud to call him brother.

There's a saying:
"You can choose your friends,
but you can't choose your family".
On this, I do agree.
But no matter what, my brother,
you are the only lifelong friend for me!
What a blessing to have been
raised together, in a loving home,
with a mother on whom we could rely.
She taught us to have a mutual love and respect;
and that is more valuable
than anything money can buy.

Thank you for the times you held my hand,
and simply said, "Sissy, it'll be alright."
Through many childhood fears,
that little saying always chased away the fright.

The childhood memories I have of us,
are sweet in every way;
but what I love the very best,
is that we are still making memories today.
And all these memories, I will hold dear,
as I do all the others.
For I cherish this precious friendship I have,

with my lifelong friend, my brother.
I Love You,
Sissy

Lovingly dedicated to Charles M. Bethune, my lifelong friend

"My Little Brother"

The day you were born, I remember well.
Both your brother and I were elated
beyond what words could even tell.
And from day one you have always been
to us, our pride and joy.
Although the year you were born was a difficult year,
God blessed us with daddy's little boy.
You were living proof to us,
that God brings beauty out of ashes.
He is faithful to bring us
joy out of mourning,
when it seems the world around us crashes.

Yes the year you were born
was also the year our father died.
Sometimes I go back in memory,
and wonder how we ever survived.
Sometimes, there are tragedies in life,
that seem too overwhelming to endure.
But God is always faithful,
to sustain us through every heartache,
as his foundation beneath us is sure.

I always feel a certain sadness,
when I think of how our father
did not live to see his youngest son;
but I know there is an eternal purpose
for everything God has done.

I have seen so much of our dad in you,
as you have grown and matured.
You walk and talk like him,
you laugh like him;
you are your father's son, for sure.

And there is no doubt
if our dad could have lived,
to see his youngest son,
he would have been just as proud of you,
as he was his oldest one.

I know God does not want us
to be consumed with the past;
but I'm glad he gave us a token of our father,
so our memory of him would vividly last.

It seems like only yesterday,
you were a quizzical young lad.
But now you are yourself a proud father,
and a proud and doting granddad.

Thank you for the joy your life has brought me.
I am so proud of the man you've become.
In my heart you have always been,
and always will be a most precious one.

There is one thing that I know for sure;
our father had two wonderful sons.
I take pride in my two brothers,
for both of my brothers are second to none.
I Love You,
Sis

Lovingly dedicated to my little brother, Herbert L. Bethune, Jr..

"Stephen"

O, precious child of God,
you were born to be raised and nurtured
by godly hands, you see:
Taught by a loving mother,
and blessed upon your grandmother's knee:
Trained up and prepared for the Master's plan
and ordained for the call that would be.

O, precious servant of God,
May I admonish you, as Paul did Timothy:
That from a child you have known Holy Scriptures,
which is able to make you wise:
Be watchful and careful in all things:
Never his chastening despise.

O, precious shepherd of God,
Feed his flock, having a ready mind:
That the aged men may be temperate and sober:
The aged women, godly and kind:
So the younger may be taught by example,
How to live a life of purity:
That the church of our Lord
May show forth a pattern of good works,
with all sincerity.

Exhort with love and patience.

Continue in the things you've been taught;
knowing that the ministry placed within,
will always come to fruition;
for nothing God does is for naught.

Remember the truths you've been assured of.
Stand firm in the faith, day by day.
For when the Chief Shepherd shall appear,
There will be much rejoicing,
in a crown of glory, that fades not away.

Dedicated to:
Rev. Stephen Black, Sr.
Pastor of Solomon's Porch Pentecostal Holiness Church,
Augusta, Ga.

Rev. and Mrs. Black are cherished co-laborers in
the ministry, and also a part of my beloved family.
I am so blessed by the ministry God has placed in them.
They are true servants of our Lord.

"A Friend I Call Sister"

I never had a sister to tell "girl things" to,
until God richly blessed my life
with a special friendship in you.
You've been a faithful, loving friend;
someone I can tell my secrets to;
always loving, caring and sharing;
a friend so kind and true.
You have smiled and laughed with me,
through the joys of life.
You have comforted me through many tears,
You have celebrated with me in many triumphs.
You have encouraged me to face my fears.
You've been a friend "who loves at all times".
You are always eager to lend a helping hand.
You always offer a shoulder to cry on.
You always seem to understand.
You have been more than a cherished friend;
you've been as a sister to me.
You are someone I depend on.
You are part of my family.
Thank you for your warm friendship.
Thank you for being someone who is kind and true.
Thank you for all you've done for me.
Thank you for just being you.

Dedicated to Carolyn A. Baughman,
a friend who is like a sister to me.

A Most Precious Blessing

When I stop to count my blessings,
to name them one by one;
I am always overwhelmed,
when I think of all that God has done!
He has blessed me with a home,
with a family and fine friends.
My many wonderful blessings
seem to go on and on, without an end!

There is a most precious blessing I am thankful for.
It's the friendship I have in you!
God has enriched my life,
by giving me a friend so kind and true!
My dear friend, you have brought me laughter.
You have put many smiles upon my face.
There are friends who come and go,
but none could ever take your place!

You have been a friend "who has loved at all times".
just as the Word says a true friend would do.
You've been a ray of sunshine,
when I've been a little blue.
When I need someone to talk to,
you lend a listening ear.
And you always offer a shoulder to cry on,
When I've needed to shed a tear.

You always reach out to others.
You exemplify the goodness
of our heavenly Father above.
Many times you have been his hand extended,
showing forth his gracious love.

Thank you for your warm friendship.
In my heart, you will always have a special place.
I thank God for the many blessings
he has given through his amazing grace.

Dedicated to Joyce Henthorn, who has been an inspiration to my
faith.

"From The Heart"

The word of our Lord teaches
that from the abundance of the heart
the mouth would speak.
And we all find this to be true.
But words spoken, still seem inadequate
to express all my gratitude to you!

My vocabulary is limited
when it comes to letting you know,
how much you both mean to me;
I've always depended on you so.

And over the years,
your faith has been as a beacon in the night
shining forth that all may see
God's love as a radiant light.

Sis, Jean, there is one sure thing
I have learned from you;
to stand firmly in the faith;
being assured that God, who has promised,
will faithfully see me through.
Yes, you have been a "mother to many";
just as the word of prophecy said you would be.
You have been lovingly teaching all of your children;
so that they might be what God would have them to be.

Pastor, may I take a moment, to let you know

all that your guidance has meant to me.
For every word of assurance,
when my faith seemed a little dim.
For every time you simply said,
"continue to trust in him."
Pastor, I thank you even for the words of correction;
for without them, where would I be?
I would not be the woman of God I am today;
so I truly want to thank you with all sincerity.

Oh how enriched and blessed my life has been
having known the both of you.
You both have been humble servants of our Lord,
standing fast in the word of truth.

Continue on in the ministry you've been assured of;
holding steadfast in the faith day by day,
For when the Chief Shepherd shall appear,
there will be much rejoicing,
in a crown of glory, that fades not away!

I Love You Both,
Leah

Lovingly dedicated to my Pastors,
Rev and Mrs. Oscar Whiteside Jr.
Living Waters Church
Augusta, Ga.

"A Mother's Prayer"

Dear Heavenly Father,

I once thought
I had to achieve and obtain so much,
to be what I needed to be.
It wasn't until I became a mother,
that I began to see;
My greatest accomplishments, in this life,
were my children;
And they were depending on me,
to lovingly teach them and to mold them
into the Godly individuals you desired them to be.

Lord, I wasn't a mother for very long,
before I realized it was a difficult task!
But there has always been a sincere request,
for which I continue to humbly ask;
Impart to me your wisdom,
and all your wisdom may bring.
I do not ask for riches or any worldly thing.

Lord, my desire is to be the mother
you would be proud of.
May my life always exemplify you.
May I seek your guidance and patience,
in all I say and do.
Fill me with all that is necessary

for my dear children to see
your steadfast love and kindness;
Lord, let it always flow through me.

I've always known there would be a time,
that you would knock
on the door of their hearts.
The greatest fulfillment as a mother
is to know, for you they've been set apart.

I know the most precious
and, yes, priceless gifts
were given to me from above.

These blessings came in the form of children
bundled in God's eternal love.
May all the days I have with them
be days I teach them of you.
May my children be a living testimony
of our Heavenly Father,
who has always been faithful and true.

Thank you for all your bountiful blessings
and for such a fine family!
May we ever walk in the light of your love,
and be all you've called us to be.

"When God Made Moms"

God has always possessed a tenderness
that he longed for mankind to see;
So he lovingly fashioned a mother's heart;
And within it,
he caused his gently attributes to be.
He placed within a mother's heart
a steadfast love much like his own.
He put his nurturing qualities inside,
of which mankind has never fully known.
He etched the smile upon a mother's face
that always shows the warmth of caring.
He lovingly placed within her hands
the magical touch of sharing.
He placed within her arms
an affectionate embrace;
And instilled in her heart, for her children,
a very special place.

"A Senior's Prayer"

Dear Heavenly Father,

When I feel as though I've outlived my usefulness,
and I fail to see for myself any purpose or goal;
May I be reminded there is always someone to minister to,
needing encouragement and hope for the soul.

If I, as Elijah, despair over life's unsettling troubles;
And I feel abandoned and on my own;
Gently shake me, and quickly remind me,
you promised to never leave me alone!

I may often feel as though I've reached the age,
of which I'm of "no earthly good"!
But, Lord, you used your servant Caleb,
simply because he knew you could!

So, Lord, help me to look beyond myself,
that I may clearly see you.
May I stand in the confidence of your word,
and in your promises, that are faithful and true.

Help me to be your hand extended
in all I may say or do;
and may my footsteps lead someone to Calvary,
to find the same friend that I found in you.

Teach me to wisely number
the remainder of my days;

that I may be a living testimony
that brings glory to you always.

Thank you, Lord, for being my rest,
when I've been weary.
Thank you for being my ever sufficient grace.
Thank you for being my shelter and my shield.
Thank you for that secret hiding place.
I even thank you for the winds of adversity,
that from time to time have blown.
For without these stormy trials,
my faith would have never grown.

Thank you, Lord, for being my all in all.
Without you, I fear to think where I'd be.
You've been that abundant joy,
and perfect peace to me.

There will be a time that I'll declare,
as the great Apostle Paul;
"I've fought a good fight, I've kept the faith";
I've given this journey in life my all!

"No Place, No Time"

Just as soon as we begin our adult journey,
and we come to understand what "work" is about;
we look forward to the time of retirement;
and we eagerly make plans for it, no doubt!

While we are young, we dream of "propping up our feet",
and spending days in total sublime!
But as we grow older and wiser,
for "slowing up", there's no place, there's no time.

When we are young and able to "kick up our feet",
and "run full-steam ahead";
just the thought of having to do too much,
always brings an enormous dread!

But as we mature and become wiser,
to squander a day, there's no reason, nor rhyme.
And for wasted days, unaccounted,
there's no place, there's no time!

God has given us the precious gift of life,
which is made up of valuable days.
May he teach us to number them wisely,
and walk pleasing to him in every way.

"THE GREATEST CHRISTMAS GIFT"

I often think of that sacred night,
so many years ago;
When God's radiant, eternal light
set the earth aglow!
How glorious and wondrous
it must have been,
as the angels bent down to see,
the perfect gift, so marvelous,
that had come to you and me.

I wonder how much Mary understood,
that solemn, star-lit night.
I wonder if she knew
she cradled earth's salvation,
as she held her little one so tight.
I wonder if she understood,
as she gazed into his precious face;
that she was beholding her Creator,
full of tender mercy and unfailing grace.

Do you suppose she could comprehend,
as she held his tiny hand;
that heaven came down
and kissed the earth.
Goodwill had come to man.

Did she know her babe would heal the sick,
and cause blinded eyes to see;
or bring hope to common mortals
as he walked the shores of Galilee?

I wonder if she understood;
do you think she had the insight to see?
One day her precious little boy
would be wounded for our transgressions,
bruised for our iniquities.

Would her heart be able to bear the harsh reality;
that he would become the sacrificial lamb,
who would die for you and me?
Did she know that one day he would walk
a lonely path up Calvary's hill;
to shoulder the burden of sin-sick man,
according to his Father's perfect will?

We will never know all that Mary understood;
Now will we fully comprehend;
the priceless, self-less sacrifice
our Lord became for man.

So at this Christmas season,
may we look beyond the tinsel, and glittering tree;
and celebrate the "Hope of All Ages"
who brought eternal life to you and me.

"The Reason For The Season"

There are folks who anticipate Christmas
for many different reasons;
putting their hopes and dreams
in many things for the season.

Some dream of preparing
just the right Christmas meal.
Some put their hopes in getting
to the right store for the greatest deals.

There are those who dream of receiving
that one perfect gift.
Oh they just know
it would give them such a lift!

Some put all their attention
on holiday décor;
trimming the house with lights,
and hanging garland on the door.

Many are diligent in finding
the most beautiful Christmas cards;
making sure they write
expressing their fondest regards.

There are those who travel far
to see their nearest kin.
Some plan special occasions,

hoping folks will drop in.

Some stay busy baking cookies,
and other delicious treats.
Some fight the crowds
to watch a parade on the city streets.

Yes, there is so much excitement
at this special time of year.
So many things to do
to bring us holiday cheer.

But in the hustle and bustle
of the Christmas Season,
may we never lose sight
of the real reason.

For Jesus is the true reason
why we are to celebrate.
He is the only one who can make
this time of year so great!

There is so much happiness
in festive things we do;
But only a Christ-centered Christmas,
will bring real joy to you!